POEMS.

BY

ANNE WHITNEY.

NEW YORK:
D. APPLETON & COMPANY,
346 & 348 BROADWAY.
1859.

CONTENTS.

JOY.

GRAY strength of years !
Whereon so many a bark is wrecked ;
And even success
Falls blank and passionless ;
This morn has decked
Your front with trailing loveliness,
And branching lights ;
Inlets of summer from celestial heights.

Dimpling with light, beneath the long arcades,
The shadows smile in sleep :
And all those forces manifold that keep
Such infantine, calm play,

Before the awful hand
That makes and breaks,
Sing and are jubilant to-day.
Sing on, all up and down the shining land !
My heart your meaning takes.

As evening's star on star,
Through the blue portals of the air,
What countless creatures throng !
And beautiful they are—
With morning in their eyes and in their hair ;
And on their lips an antique speech and song.

One shadow only waits
Aloof, poised on ascending wing,
And lifts no voice ; but in her throat,
I ween there is a sweeter note
Than all these glorious warblers bring.
I hear her chant an inward strain ;
" Thou sett'st me above Time's annoy :

I found delight and it was pain ;
Thou gavest pain, and it is joy.
Token of unaccomplished growth,
Stern pledge of immortality ;
Through all the earth's perplexed domain,
Just God ! I would that there should be
No living thing that should not suffer PAIN."
Thus in a ravishment
Of inward sight, her song wells up,
A passionate content.

Scatter the road,
The beaten highway of the world, my heart,
With rose and asphodel,
And all thou draw'st from music's throbbing well ;
Behold how rich thou art !
Thou drink'st of every spring of God ;
Broad heaven but lightly freights thine eye,
And thy familiar pulse is rife
With tumult of the river of life,

That makes the circuit of the youngest sky.
What thrill that spirits feel,
Transport of love, or ecstasy
Of still, creative force,
That life shall not at last to thee reveal?

O make no barren haste—
Thou livest from day to day with God so near!
And well may'st brook
Into those phantom-eyes to look
That freeze in these half-lights our atmosphere:—
Seeing that thou art based
On the immortal Joy—whose spreading bloom
Hath root of substance so divine,
That the perennial heavens which by it shine,
And spring's sure birth, live only to express
Its strength and everlastingness.

THE CEYBA AND THE YAGUEY.

Know you the land?
With its cestus of summer waves, and its ocean
Of young, soft air, with a vernal motion
All through its golden tides? which caresses
And busies itself about you, and blesses
All that it bathes with life ineffable,
A breathing of infinite love, as well
As of courage and youth? That joy of the sun
Where heaven in all its beauty is won
To the arms of the new-made earth—do you know it?
That land of hope—that land of the poet?

There in that isle, as you shall hear,
The Ceyba grows—of godlike cheer;

A sad and singular history
Is that of the beautiful Ceyba-tree,
And what I recount of one alone,
Is true of a thousand as of one.

Grand and alone the giant stood,
The Ceyba-tree of royal mood.
It stood so great that the careless Montero
Of the sunny Partido de Sumidero,
Cheering his mules with song and whistle,
Winding about those mountains that bristle
With cactus outré, and pine, and yucca,
And soften as well with twining bejuca,
And the delicate weft of the tamarind
Afloat on the sunny tropic wind,
Seeing afar in the freshening skies,
This beacon of silent centuries,
Touched his cap in the way of his nation,
Making his morning salutation.
The giant, I said, of royal heart,

Kept with his sky and his earth apart.
Truly, it mattered not if beneath
The laurel upwafted proud, full breath,
And the spiked aloe's wondrous bloom
Enriched the warm, deep under gloom,—
Far and forgetful the whispering Jove
Swayed in the mighty Joy above!
The cedar dwarfed in his ancient face,
The queenly Palms, from their azure dais,
Looked upward unto the Ceyba-tree;
Chestnut and mango dreamily
Heaved their soft billows in mid air,
The cypress companioned with them there,
But over them, an under sky
Of shifting emerald, airily
The Ceyba's coronal tossed and swung.

Proud songs the lofty minstrel sung!
Awful it was when the southern blast
From the sea, drove inland gray and fast,

And heavy with its terrible rain
From the chaos of the heavens and main,
(After the weary, weary drouth,
The gush of the burning-hearted south !)
To hear the inspired monarch Tree
Roar its giant hymn of Liberty :
As if it saw red morn beneath
The dim horizon's misty wreath,
Coming the dank old gloom to fuse,
And dripping with its crimson dews,
And to the world sang o'er and o'er
" Her fiery drops earth counts no more !
The hearts you shut from hope and light,
And Beauty and the Infinite,
Into the air, into the day,
Will burst their wild, indignant way ! "
Then in the calm, the light, the glory,
Most tender was its rhymed story ;
When distant and faint the unweary sea
Rolled landward its vast harmony,

And the Ceyba listened by stars and moon,
And softly answered it rune for rune.

But alas for the stately Tree! indeed
Alas for it! a little seed
Bedded itself in the cloven bark,
Nor did the generous Ceyba mark
What life it gave, what strength went forth
Into the thing of little worth!

Soon under the leaves might you espy,
Gliding and creeping silently
Forward from its buried root,
A wavering, young and snakelike shoot,
That little by little, day after day,
Twists and winds its quiet way,
'Mid shrinking leaves and buds that pine,—
And so, with many a hideous twine
Round tender twig, and bough, and branch,
Till one by one they bare and blanch,

While downward it drops an hundred feet,
And as many arms coil up and meet
And clasp the giant, neck and limb,
And strain him in their embrace with grim
And deadly love ; and here and there
Under the sick'ning foliage, peer
Keen heads like serpents' heads, intent,
And new, strange hues flop insolent
From bough to bough, till one might see
How ill it fared with the noble tree !
How, breathless and with eager strain,
Out of its falling mantle, in vain
It lifted its hundred wasted hands
To the sun and the winds, and the journeying bands
Of sky-immortals ; 'las ! the dead moon shone
On the peering serpents' heads alone,
Or flecked it with many a ghastly fleck—
The sun glared in on the spectral wreck
Unmindful, and fierce, and wonderingly :
And then the life-blood drearily

Curdled within its veins and stopt ;
While over it the Yaguey dropt
Its mocking wreaths of gaudy hue,
Flaunting triumphant in the blue,
Sweet breath of heaven, and all was done ;
And so of a thousand as of one.

A LAST DREAM.

Three against one! Three giants it was plain—
While I might scarcely dot our battle ground,
Which glimmered east and west, and north and south,
Farther than eye might see. But all the while,
For I was sinewed by our God himself,
I knew that I should conquer. And I quailed
No jot, who shudder now, even but to think
What secret, deadly and remorseless ways
They took to break me. For one covered o'er
With his vast hand, heaven's gracious breadth of light,
That terror-stricken in the ghastly fields,
My heart might burst and die. One slowly sucked
The life blood at its fount; and from my brain

The healthy vigor went, and in its place
There was a motley whirl of fantasies,
A dreadful dance of wicked things, that struck
Strange gleams and painful lightnings through my lids
Which still I saw upon the midnight snow,
Mingling with pure auroras from the bergs,
And meteors' silver flashes. And one—one
Loaded these limbs with dull, invisible chains,
So subtilly imposed, so stern and still,
It seemed to lull the will into accord,
And hoodwink all my soul with trust. But no!
I rose, I strove with triple giant strength,
And heaved, as earthquakes mountains from their
shoulders,
The settling weights away, and heard them slide
Into that night of sound, that northward far,
Where the white sea-gull flies, for leagues on leagues,
Wraps in its shadowy arms the gleaming coast.
Loathing and shuddering, at length I drew
The clinging fury from my heart—and lo!

Not overhead, I think, nor from the east,
Where the sun has its solemn, annual birth,
Nor glazing the waste whiteness, nor unsheathing
The glaciers' keen swords,—but fine and still,
And as it seemed, dilating from a seed
Of light within,—light peaceful, broad and soft,
Grew round me where I stood. And God, who watched
The battle from his trembling depths of Night,
In sign and seal of this my victory,
Sends his calm angel here, who folds an arm
About and leads me safe, I ask not where,
For heart and life are pillowed on his love.

Will any say, I yielded,—drawing near
Those lists of high renown, where the gaunt Three
And I fought the dumb battle out, and left
No trace in the blown, desert fields?—Nay, far
Beyond the last low wall of crimson light,
That struggles to hedge off with baby gleam,
The insurging Dark,—where sits the sceptred cold

Impassible and still, and the awed sea
Groans only and upheaves in marble waves,
When the black sleet-wind whispers, Mutiny!
There is a shaft, as all the world may know,
A monument of ice uptowering dim
Into the heavens' crowned mystery—whereon
Are graven with touches of the light, a name,
And following that, a chronicle of deeds.
And when the brief, high history makes end,
The page of ice goes on—" And one day, Earth,
Gray mother, bound with frost and torn with fire,
Shall surely be redeemed by hero dust.
Each sluggish atom of her sphere, shall bloom
Nobly in human shape, and take the print,
And do the mandate of a godlike will,
Until her apotheosis be won.
Dear then to her and to the silent Powers,
And borne on their strong wings above defeat,
And fear of mockery, all they who build
In stern emprise a shrine for the Unseen;

Making life poor to show how rich it is.
Round them heaven's flaming currents stoop and play,
And lap the stifling vapors of the world,
Till the space freshens into festal depths ;
And Soul, before a royal mendicant,
Pensioned of flesh along her dusky way,
Goes forth with bounty to exultant crowds,
With pulse of music ordering the winds,
And trumpets blowing the eternal morn.
And so to guard from loss and blight of Time
The memory of such faith, and of a will
That thrilled our adamant from coast to coast,
This pale resplendent pillar of the frost
Scores the dark, grasping air. But he who held
Within his eyes, the sacred fire that pierced
Our ancient mysteries, and laid them bare
Behind their five-fold barriers, afar
Wins smiles from other heavens, and breathes the meed
Of mighty toils—the insatiate sweet of rest."

Be it then—rest. All round the scented coast
Flashes the living sea ; and on my brow
I feel the silken touches of strange winds ;
While overhead such light, and sumptuous blue,
And rustle of great plumes ! Still thought toils on
In memory :—and over me those words
That kindle the wild gleam around, throb out :
And still I hear an under voice which says,
That what we do is better than ourselves,
Being held unto the service of His will
By the strong hand that fashioned us. Even so.
But by that stair I climb to God at last,
Trampling on ease and low usurping wants ;
And through innumerable spheres upreaching,
And Nights and Days till I am lost in Him.

FIVE SONNETS RELATING TO BEAUTY.

I.

I DREAMED an angel, Angel twice, through death,
Wrought us another "Night." A stately dream,
Where reconciling Infinites did seem
To fold round life's perplexities, and wreath
Its ancient glooms with stars :—a marble breath
From Art's serene, fresh, everlasting morn,
Where the dull worm of earthly pain is born
To winged life thenceforth, and busieth
With golden messages its mortal hours.
O the Divine, earth would have wronged and slain !
Its pangs are rays above her falling towers
Of lovelier truth—breaths of a sweet disdain
Shedding strange nothingness on meaner pain,
Drops of the bleeding god that turn to flowers.

II.

Largess from seven-fold heavens, I pray, descend
On all who toil for Beauty! Never feet
Grow weary that have done her bidding sweet
About the careless world! For she is friend
And darling of the universe;—and day by day,
She comes and goes, but never dies,
So precious is she in the eternal eyes.
O dost thou scorn her, seeing what fine way
She doth avenge? For heaven, because of her,
Shall one day find thee fitter. How old hours
Of star-rapt night about thy heart had curled—
And thou hadst felt the morning's golden stir,
And the appealing loveliness of flowers,
Yea, all the saving beauty of the world!

III.

O fair mistrust of earth's more solid shows !
And mute appeal from its inhuman ways,
Its iron judgments and its misspent praise,
To the appreciation sweet that glows
In heaven's old smiling eye ! O slowly grows
Our human thought ; and freedom long delays,
Love in the shade fulfilling weary days,
Ere her great child is born ! No wasting throes
Foretell thy being to the universe !
It is as thou didst lurk on half-poised wings
Below our life, blessing, and care and curse,
Even at the very root and core of things :
And couldst not keep from start, and chirp, and flight,
And warbled hint of something back of sight.

IV.

No slight caprice rules thee.—Who sounds one note
In God's high order finds thee at his side.
Thou art twin-born with joy, and dost abide
With conscience old, and blood-deep art inwrought
With love's sweet mystery. No wanton thought
Shall wrong the world that holds thee, or the wide
Deep Ordering, whereof thou art the bride.
For neither hate, nor custom's stress, nor aught
Of evil can thee harm, divinest thing ;
And through these folds of sense, thou openest
Blue rifts to Freedom and unfathomed rest.
Flower of a hidden life, sweet mystic spring,
What joy must tune thy flow, and calm divine !
What soundness at the heart from east to west !

V.

And for that thou art Beauty, and thy name
Transcends all praise of thee, and doth but leave
Thyself for thy true rendering, I grieve
O'er idle words. O never dost thou blame,
But seekest to inspire me all the same,
With thine immortal freshness! Through the night
The moon comes large and slow, winging with light
The joyous sea; while sunset's last red flame,
Baring the heavens for glories to succeed,
Goes softly out, with endless farewell gleams,
Ebbing along the yellow marge of day;
Glides slow, with backward gaze; sadly indeed,
And slow, as from the heart which new love claims
An older memory doth steal away.

HYMN TO THE SEA.

Along yon soft tumultuousness, the Dawn
  Reaches a glowing hand, and the mute world
  Thrills back to life. This lustrous blossom, curled
In on its dreaming heart, feels the forlorn
Old Shadow lift, and guardedly discloses
Its wayside cheer ; and endless waves away
    Bide the slow triumph of the Light,
    Rejoicing in the infinite
  And quenchless possibility of Day ;
Day,—that at least shall win far more than darkness
  loses.

Over those morning waves, or when the bare
  Stars glow, or Moon her tireless lover nears,

The eternal Beauty that these countless years
Makes earthly musings so divinely fair,
Broods listening to the prophecy thou chantest—
The subtle breath of mortal sympathies
Is she, wooing us unto right
In unsuspected ways ; a light
From inmost heaven tempered to dreaming eyes,
A sweet foreshadow of the joy for which thou pantest.

Roll in from far thy deep broad-skirted thunder,
Whereon the wild winds fawn! *Thy* voice by day—
But Night adopts and trances it away
Into its clear, sad universe of wonder.
O weary of life's lavish, shallow sound,
Enrich me beyond hunger with that tone!
Tell in what deep, gray solitude,
It may be born, what caverns rude
Still haunt it ; and if the infinite ALONE
Touch it himself with calm and utterance so profound.

Hark'ning through all the music of her leaves
And inland murmurs, o'er the seaward steep,
The stately Summer leans, while dim winds sweep
Her shining tresses back—and half she grieves
That thou disdain'st with thy hoar wreaths, to twine
Her fleeting gifts.—Yet hast thou tender fancies ;
Broodings of love when young winds cease,
And silence deepens into peace ;
And leadest with Day and Night immortal dances,
Crowned with fresh marriage-blooms and lotus-cups
divine.

Upon the broad, gray, gleaming beach I saw,
Last night, that phantom-light of thy desire,
Orb large and slow in the East, dropping pale fire
Along thy deep'ning tumult, so to draw
Old love-dreams out :—for countless leagues she
had come
O'er kindred foam ; her footfalls echoing yet
In the deep breast of Aral—through

Caspian and Euxine, and the blue
Of that famed gulf in earth's broad girdle set,
With endless voice of waves calling to shores long
dumb.

With all her loveliness earth leaves me sad,
And sadder for her loveliness. My hills
Are sacred chalices which eve o'erfills
With vintage for young gods ; and deeply glad
In the sweet clasp of vernal boughs, the air
At night-fall swoons ;—but hauntings unexplained
Steal in ; earth looks half wild and lone,
And from her eyes I veil my own,
And lay my heart to hers—the unattained,
Youth's aching world of incompleteness throbbing
there.

But thou, shout on through heaven's soft, circling
spheres,
Still promising with that great voice of power

A joy to every heart, a day, an hour
To come, outweighing all these silent years!
Afar thou veil'st thy kingliness in mist,
And stretchest in the heaven's most deep embrace,
Like the great Future, waste and gray,
Dissolving day to yesterday—
But what fair shores thou lapp'st in azure peace!—
What isles of joyous palms with tropic starlight kissed!

I am borne outward by this fragrant breeze,
That seems to press its warm lips to the sand,
And then away, beyond the singing land,
To that hoar silence of the lone mid seas,
Where thou, in unrelated strength, a bare
Vast heart, throbbest beneath the eternal eye:—
Life soars like an enfranchised flame;
The needy doubt, the hope, that came
Before the laggard dawn to wake me, fly,
And dim Eternity flows in like silent air.

Do tempests swing thee, or deep, choral nights
 Chant unto murmurous slumber, yield me still
 The calm of hushed abysses!—human ill
Patience transfigures on her visioned heights.
Thou dost not rive the blood-drenched deck apart,
Nor whelm the slaver's freight of woes, but soft
  On patient, swelling breast upborne,
  Waftest the dismal burthen on,
As trusting in the love that waits aloft,
And the slow germ of good in man's unquiet heart.

Ah, meagre happiness, and hopes that reach
 To some dull dream, a vapor of the sense,
 And on the plain of the old Permanence
Are but as hasty flashes in the beach
Of idle footprints! O make more divine
Glad Sea, our thoughts—nor may we dully grope
  'Mid slavish fears, while thou dost girth
  The continents and isles with mirth,
And music of unconquerable hope

That Joy and Beauty shall be earth's as they are
thine!

O old consoler, that dost tenderly
In thy great longing merge my day-born pain,
Uplift me to the stature of your strain,
And bid all lower aspiration flee!
The nobler earth is built of stubborn good—
Who brings his little vanity, his grave
Appeal to men's applause and wonder,
Warn him away with thy hoarse thunder,
Flash o'er the graven sands a liberal wave,
And let us know no more name, memory, or blood!

And call the regal shadows, 'mid the roar
Of charging waves, the tumult and the smoke,—
That fine old Grecian in his threadbare cloak;
The banner pastor by blue Zurich, o'er
Whose vine-clad summits Alps looked not in vain;
England's blind seer; Toussaint, the kingly heart

Wearing his thrice-earned martyr crown ;
And all who silently let down
The rugged slopes whereon we toss apart
Some herald-beam of the All-Fair, some love-bought pain.

Yet milder beams wooing the folded sight,
Shed warmth far down in many a sunless nook :
Thank God, there are no eyes in which we look
But some heart's love doth lend them beauteous light !
Dreams that prefigure hopes, and hopes that take
Fresh courage from all life ; from starlight bold
Sung softly in by whip-poor-wills,
And sunset's broad'ning sails o'er hills
Afar ; and from the earth that grows not old,
Float lightly o'er our heads whether we sleep or wake.

Alas ! to her high place thro' sea-deep tears,
Earth wins her long, slow, agonizing way !

The base, triumphant Despot of a day
Is weary Anarch of a thousand years.
And yet this many a spring the boughs are sheen
With the almost forgotten bloom! Call, Sea,
Unto all faithful souls, Doubt not,
Aspire to lead earth's struggling thought
Still up, bring what from full hearts gushes free,
He who doth blend and shape the whole finds nothing mean.

When morning, loosing from its crimson drifts,
Some panting skylark overtakes, most tender
Of such weak rivalship, and prone to render
Homage unto great-heartedness, it lifts
The breaking strain, and all along its lines
Of thrilling light, its currents of pure air
And rosy mists, winds it at will,
Unites and separates, and still
Wreathes it and builds anew beyond despair,
Till light is song, song light thro' all heaven's steadfast

O know how all things change! Night's violet star
Bloomed red erewhile; and thou, Sea, wearest away
The glorious realm of a forgotten day,
But lay'st the pillars of a fairer far
Deep in thy caverned bed; for all that ever
Gathered about it men's delight or love,
Or aught that simply blooms, or strives
To make more beautiful our lives,
In each new fabric of the world, is wove
Afresh, and changes like the light, but passes never.

K. F.

You are welcome, world, to censure and carp:
Sing and croak yourselves hoarse if you will;
'Tis pleasant to find 'mid blame and praise,
One who is sweet and stable still.

What! you don't see that it's all in vain?
That Madame will neither be you nor I:
But simply herself; God bless her for that!
And grant us to prize her accordingly!

TWO STANZAS.

Seem I beyond thy reach of eye
Or lip, mailed in the arrogance
Of life?—O friend, withhold no glance
Of love or word of courtesy!

Ponder with carefulness, and own
All win as thou—are as thou art—
Think of the beggar in the heart—
Think what the silent stars have known.

TASSO.

How darkly in the far silence
Of my pitiless prison-walls,
I through the night-watches sit !

High over me speed Orion,
The seven stars and Aldebaran,
Sirius and the twin beauteous gods.

Radiant in celestial spaces,
Beautiful, and free, and peaceful,
As calm as the pure heart of God !

Ye winds, that have leave to wander
Deep into remotest heavens,
Waft me to those glad spheres.

Far from the terrible noises,
And stillness yet more terrific,
Wild with its dread interruptions.

Might I, for an hour behind me,
Leave the long-eating anguish and fear—
Yes, O God ! the madness—

And feel the cool touch of midnight,
And the dew's most fresh benediction,
And the freedom of life—of life !

Away 'mid the purple bloom
Of the hills, the south wind is strengthened
With the sweet, wild vigor of pine.

The rock meets the fern's soft caress,
And that flower that meek salutation
Sends starward, looks timid to earth.

Ah ! the lark in the cloud-rack bathes,
And drinks at the air's still fountains,
And is he not thirstless and pure ?

O for life that is life !—

Joy in being ; hopes o'er-filling
The blessed to-day with to-morrow,
Faith, the queenly, that rules all hap ;

Love, the ever-compassionate,
The dear love of man and of woman,
That affection whose sweets hide no sting !

O bitter ! that ever the heart,
Still asking impossible treasure,
Should cast from it aught that is loving !

Dear heart of my mother, mother
Long resting from earth and anguish,
Pity—pity, pity thy child !

O what have they taken from me ?
Thought, and will, and affection,
And left for my brain but a throb,

For my heart but endless thirsting,
And the blank, burnt desert of being
Spread awful, and blinding, and mute.

Yet sometimes in the great Presence
Of moments fallen from heaven,
Whose law, though not known, I obey,

Once more is thought disentangled,
And there come the beautiful children
Of the eternal spring unto me.

O welcome then anguish and pain,
And welcome bitter oppression!
Am I mad then?—so let me remain.

THE PROSPECT.

O WONDROUS delight of a window
  A fair three stories high,
With its view to the southward and west,
  And its limitless boon of sky!

With its murmur and coo of pigeons,
  Settling upon the roof—
And a distant stir that betokens
  A world that is well aloof!

And here when the heavens are azure,
  And no dunce that you know is near
To hint at a weather-breeder,
  In the magical atmosphere ;

When swallows on cleaving pinions,
  Disdaining the earth and you,
Follow the hunt far up
  In the calm, embosoming blue ;

Or when in the west mount Prospect
  Indues its purple ; and ah !
When my planet looks down on the mill-stream
  My porphyro-genita ;

I look with a half enchantment
  Over regions that wait renown,
The triple crest of Waltham,
  And vales of Watertown ;

Over orchard, and woodland, and meadow,
Where the Beaver its raving stills,
O'er fair little ups and downs
To the mighty, girdling hills.

What silence of expectation—
What dreaming on the to-come,
When up through these valleys and hillsides
Yon hive shall swarm and hum!

For yonder, beyond our paling
Of elm, and ash, and oak,
Hangs soft on the purple distance
A visible, brooding smoke;

There, masked in brick, Trimountain
Rears somewhat snobbish and chill,
But returns in its way the salute
Of oak-crowned Meetinus hill

But here, while I may, I am laughing
  To think how pleasant a thing,
To fly to this skiey quiet,
  And freshen a ruffled wing.

My poverty and its vexations
  Vanish and leave me free :—
From Cushing's, inclusive, eastward
  To the feet of the journeying sea ;

From the hither wall of Barnard
  To Knobscot's blue recess—
Through lands of Locke to the south
  With acres more or less,

In the yield of all farms and woodlands,
  We, Robin and I, go shares ;
And our landlords are sunbeams and waters,
  And grudge us no repairs.

Ah world, if you yet must have me,
Sing me a better strain,
Or hold me a moment, I pray,
Lightly, and loose me again.

THE BRIDGE OF THE DRAGON.

GODLIKE is goodness !—evermore serene,
  And young, and prodigal of lovely days !
A touch of magnanimity where men are mean,
  A vestal thought in earth's polluted ways,
Forgiveness, grateful as the oak's large green,
  A generous faith in one who errs, like rays
Surviving the lost star, for ever make
A bubbling in the desert for our sake.

And so, most glad, I turn from the unreal,
  Sad shows of life, impatient lips to wet
At an old well of freshness ; to that leal
  Sweet vision of St. Margaret ; may she yet

Restore to many a heart its lost ideal,
  And help me for some moments to forget,
Borne on the cooling stillness of the dream,—
How the loud multitude without blaspheme !

Might it have been at such an hour as this,
  An autumn eventide, that Margaret said :
"God binds his ancient world to perfectness,
  Veined is every wind-flower with faint red,
Five petals must the wild-brier have, no less ;
  And in the cavern's black and silent shade,
The hoar rocks flower, like lilies in bright air,
The secret'st thoughts of God are all so fair !"

Through arching boughs, o'er which the clematis
  Tosses its misty curls, and woodbines run,
A wandering flame, and grapes swing, not the less
  For ivy near, glooms goldenly the sun,
As through an old church-window ;—if I miss
  The pictured saints, the sounds immortal, won

From fields of silence, yet be this the glory
Leading me to those quaint days, and to my story!

Summer was flaunting wide, when sudden blight
  Paled all; the leaf, the grain, the autumn fruit
Set in the stalk; as on a perfect night
  The nightingale, mid-song, struck sudden mute.
Margaret, in sad disquiet at the sight,
  Wept for her people, wept for the poor brute
Chained to the stall: alas! and none could tell
What malady it was which thus befell.

Wild, they implored the saints—the Christ, all pale,
  All powerful, drooping from the awful rood;—
But ah, what dismal, broken-hearted wail
  Was there—what bitter freezing in the blood,
When tidings came, that prone across their vale,
  Long leagues away in the primeval wood,
With breath secreting pestilential dew,
His hideous bulk of ill, the Dragon threw!

They sought in vain to reason of their ill.
  Frantic were some, and cried bewildered :
" We are but playthings of Almighty will."—
  " Take we our flocks and cattle," others said,
" And last year's hoardings of the press and mill ;
  Alas ! what fruitful valley lies ahead,
Or whither shall we go, that pestilence
And aching famine may not follow hence ? "

They called to mind the ancient prophecy
  That in the fiery Dragon's rule abhorred,
The first year, blight would take the grain, and dry
  The honey juices, which their orchards stored ;
But if another spring, his ghastly sigh
  Came curdling up the wind, shedding abroad
Its sick, hoar vapors, far more dreadful blight
On man and beast, and on the earth would light.

Ere then, dead seers had said, worse loss will be,
  Than loss of corn and wine :—of noble dower

In knightly skill and gentle courtesy,
 Of states' parental care :—a bitter hour
Of helpless tears and low-lipped mockery ;
 When thought is low, and all abroad a power
Of subtle evil rife, and few aware,
And vernal-hearted men fail everywhere.

At morn they celebrate the solemn mass.
 In the thin light, wan look the choristers,
And wan the priest—a piteous sight, alas !
 But heart-like, tenderly, the music stirs
And throbs ; and keen, strong-winged, doth overpass
 The large-eyed multitude upon the floors,
'Mid the all-powerful relics, bending low,
And 'neath St. Catherine's heaven-illumined brow.

On Margaret's lids that saintly radiance stole,
 As in the pauses of the holy chaunt,
Like a continued harmony, her soul
 Went on in thought ;—as if some ministrant

And heavenly joy were given for earthly dole,
  O'er lids and brow it spread—like streams that haunt
The northern stars, waving in dreamy play,
And warmed her kneeling shadow all away.

To her it seemed, that from celestial height,
  The good St. Catherine leaned, and said, Dear child,
The Virgin pure, mother of godlike might,
  Teaches the loving heart and undefiled,
All it shall do; have faith in that far light!
  Surely it was no dream, surely she smiled,
And bending over her still further, lo!
She kissed her warm eyelids, and kissed her brow.

The noble music softly pined away:—
  And, hiding in her bosom's blameless pride,
The glittering rosary, upon her way
  Went Margaret forth: the heavens no good denied,

No omen sweet; transparent shone the day,
  And rich with flowings of the summer tide:—
"But earth is sick," she mused, "she takes no heed;"
And through her brain thoughts ran with crimson speed.

From day to day more grievous waxed their bale,—
  Weeks passed and months, nor any comfort brought;
Like one who treads a death-room, cold and pale,
  With velvet pace the light stole in and out;
There was no winged joy—no insect wail—
  No hum of little life always about;
Till summer wasted by, and from the north
The fierce gales blew, and drove the monster forth.

Brief joy! brief hope! sad breathing space for those
  Who but take breath to meet the coming toil!
"When May returns," they cried, "with the early rose,
  Jesus us save, and God our sins assoil!
All hope is gone from us, all dear repose,
  For guilty have we been, we may not foil

Just doom." So winter passed, and roaring March,
And April came, quick glimmering through God's arch.

Ah, what a joy !—along fresh winking rills,
  Crept the young green : the swallows, many a one,
Turned their far-travelled wings, and daffodils
  Were merry in the heart-reviving sun.
The wind-flower pale and violet o'er the hills
  Found footing here and there, and every dun,
Stark limb and twig emitted its soft flame ;
And this was May, and with the rose she came.

Did then the o'erburthened winds of May-time rave ?
  Or little daisies babble as they reeled ?
Or came the word on some elysian wave,
  That, to a maiden it had been revealed
How, praise to Christ, she might her people save ?
  Alone would she go forth through wood and field,
And passing o'er the dragon's fallen pride,
Meet them in joy upon the further side.

And they believed. Ah, blessed to believe!
  In gentleness, in love outwearying fate,
In Mary, mother, ever to believe!
  O love, be conquered never by old hate!
No noble heart of its sweet faith bereave!
  The world is watching at your palace-gate
With various eyes, and all the Past crowds here,
And all the Future waits with anxious fear.

When the first taint in May's delicious breath,
  Warned them to part, with hopeful steps apace,
They journeyed forth. Stranger, and kin, and kith,
  Slow age, and childhood with its supple grace,
And thoughtful prime, and infancy therewith,
  Depart to skirt the mountain's shadowy base,
And resting off the monster's further side,
Watch from afar what fortune should betide.

Then Silence reigned, that ancient Eremite!
  And Margaret from her dwelling, as a star,

Awakes upon some softly-bosomed night,
  Came forth : no evil taint her path might mar ;
The May winds breathed about her their delight ;
  The heavens spread broad and calm, they looked
      not far ;
With all their depth, their old, mysterious birth,
They seemed to be the feeling of the earth.

Along the valley, green, and warm, and soft,
  A fresh-leaved myrtle-branch in hand, she went ;
Mildly the sober people of the croft
  Gazed after her ; the little skylark lent
A soul to the embracing blue, and soon aloft
  The antique wood leaned over her, attent,
And dropped its pictured glooms upon her fair,
White-gleaming vesture and her shining hair.

What thoughts her angel steps accompanied !
  Grave legends, fragrant of the olden time ;

Tales of heroic worth, and faith or deed
  Smooth tuned unto some sweet, immortal rhyme :—
But, dearest to her heart, were thoughts which fed
  Its anxious hope—of patient love, sublime
In noiseless triumph over force and hate,
And brutal wrath, and lusts intemperate.

She was with noble Daniel, given o'er
  Unto like shaggy doom ; and, unaware
Her busy heart conceived him evermore,
  As beautiful, with heavenly look, and air
By deathless youth upborne. Still memory bore
  Unto her side, true saints enshrined there,—
Heroes of life-long patience and pure will,
Who kept her heart to its calm centre still.

Through the green darkness thus she journeyed on.
  The sun went down, the brightness fled away
From the warm west, as when one dies, anon
  From brow to heart the white eclipse makes way,

And for the time a sadder grace is won,
  So ebbed the crimson current of the day
To its great, vanished heart ; and over all
Looked forth the stars—far, still, ethereal.

She rested her in many a haunted woof
  Of song, and dews, and light, and shadows shifting,
As the blithe company of leaves aloof
  Danced in the fragrant night-winds calm uplifting.
Sometimes through azure chasms, in the thick roof
  High overhead, the kindling moon went drifting
In masses of white light on banks of gloom,
Or shimmering Albeles rich with sudden bloom.

And if the clouds swelled gloomily, and sent
  Their fever-tongues into the cool, dark air,
That shrined her brightness in its moving tent,
  They harmed her not :—as nature everywhere
Had dreamed a human dream, whereso she went,
  All things breathed peace. So wondrous night did
    wear

Into white dawn, the dawn to early day,
And in her path the mighty serpent lay.

All morning-fresh, like a new-fallen thought
  From God's deep life, stood she. She felt the jar,
The air with freaks of flame, with hiss, and spot
  Staining the amber dawn, and blood-red bar,
All elfinly alive : but she saw not,
  Nor ever on him looked ; she saw afar
Her breathless people through the hiss and flame,
Their babes uplifted towards her as she came.

A moment to her heart crept the chill frost.
  One shrinking foot she set on that huge ill,
A sunbeam on a dead trunk, century-mossed ;
  One step—another and another still !—
Gasping, as he would lick her hand, all lost,
  His head upturned ;—she passed, and prone he fell
As the glad day came in—death's dull, blue veil
Settling o'er all his limbs and rainbow mail.

EVENING.

THE sun has dropped down through the west ;
  And twilight deepens on :—
A wink and a pale wink, here and there,
  So the stars come, one by one.

A thoughtful life is a pleasant life—
  Yea—dreams in a wild-brier lane ;
The air soft kindling with the moon
  Midway of her stately reign.

Where the broad light lies wavelessly,
  Where the toiling sun has lain,
A tree and its shadow, wondrous still,
  Ruling the grassy plain!

The river to the distant sea,
  Murmuring, murmuring goes;
Type of a life that broods and sings
  On unto its quiet close.

Keen firefly in the barberry shade,
  That warm'st it with such busy light,
Bear with me—rest is deeper life,
  The centering of faith and might.

Thanks—that along the shifting sands,
  As moves our sleepless tent,
Moments of higher calm are given,
  And of more true content!

Content ; the world falls off, and leaves
  A measure nobler grained,
By which I try the seeming lost,
  As well as seeming gained.

Beauty that fillest, why makest sad ?
  Thou hast no want, no haste ;
Is it that thou o'erflowest my soul,
  And I lament the waste ?

Dear heart, whose pulses with my own
  Keep their mysterious move,
That fillest every transient pause,
  With music of thy love ;

Art not thou patient too to-night,
  Divining what true strength,
What life is ours, what joy to come,
  And far-off calm at length ?

BERTHA.

THE leaves have fallen from the trees,
For under them grew the buds of May;
And such is constant Nature's way;
Let us accept the work of her hand:
If the wild winds sweep bare the height,
Still something is left for heart's delight—
Let us but know and understand.

Bertha looked from the rocky cliff,
Whose foot the tender foam-wreaths kissed—
Towards the outer circle of mist
That hedged the old and wonderful sea;

Below her as if with endless hope,
Up the beach's marbled slope,
The waters clomb unweariedly.

Many a long-bleached sail in sight,
Hovered awhile, then flitted away
Beyond the opening of the bay.
Fair Bertha entered her cottage late :
"He does not come," she said, and smiled,
"But the shore is dark and the sea is wild,
And, dearest Father, we still must wait."

She hastened to her inner room,
And silently mused there alone :
"Three springs have come—three winters gone,
And still we wait from hour to hour ;
But earth waits long for her harvest time,
And the aloe, in the northern clime,
Waits an hundred years for its flower.

"Under the apple boughs as I sit
In May-time, when the robin's song
Thrills the odorous winds along,
The innermost heaven seems to ope—
I think, though the old joys pass from sight,
Still something is left for heart's delight—
For life is endless and so is hope.

"If the aloe wait an hundred years ;
And God's times are so long, indeed,
For simple things, as flower and weed,
That gather only the light and gloom,—
For what great treasures of joy and dole,
Of life, and death perchance, must the soul
Ere it flower in heavenly peace, find room !

"I see that all things wait in trust,
As feeling afar God's distant ends—
And unto every creature, he sends

That measure of good that fills its scope :
The marmot enters the stiffening mould,
And the worm its dark, sepulchral fold,
To hide there with its beautiful hope."

Yet Bertha waited on the cliff,
To catch the gleam of a coming sail,
And the distant whisper of the gale
Winging the unforgotten home :—
And hope at her yearning heart would knock,
When a sunbeam on a far-off rock
Married a wreath of wandering foam.

Was it well ? *you* ask—(nay, was it ill ?)
Who sat last year by the old man's hearth,—
The sun had passed below the earth,
And the first star locked his western gate—
When Bertha entered her darkening home,
And smiling, said : "He does not come,
But, dearest Father, we still can wait ! "

SUSANNA.

WEARY Sea,
Spare us your dull monotony!
Up in the noble hill-land are we,
Unto its breezes we trust our fame—
Nothing here is weary or tame.

What jubilant springs these hills have greened—
What silent snows have intervened—
What magical summers over them leaned—
What autumns lighted the sombre wood,
And crimsoned it, as with its own heart's blood!

The wife of Ernest, in yonder hut,
Will tell you how many years have put
Their green on the oak, and dropped the nut,
Since this tall grove of walnut-trees
Shook their young tresses in the breeze.

The mountain-spring sings down this way,
Through night and twilight into day ;—
She told me how many inches, the play
Of the frolicsome waters, had spread,
Since first she knew it, the narrow bed.

I said to her, " Mother, 'tis well
In such fixed peace as yours to dwell ;
No sad mutation you chronicle ;
Nothing is stable within my range,
But the stern, old principle of change."

She was stooping over her herbs in the grass—
Snake-root, and flag, and sassafras,
Winter-green and—you know—a mass

Of fragrant rubbish,—as the bent mast rears,
She uplifted her eighty years.

She pointed to her hut by the wood—
Sixty years and more it has stood,
Very lowly, you see, and rude—
"Much the same is that windy shell,
As when Ernest and I went there to dwell.

"Young were we both, with little care ;
While he went out to hunt the bear,
I kept the hearth or took my share
In the garden-work—till Ernest was given,
And Mary and Jane by gracious Heaven.

"I thought God's singers I should not hear,
Or the locusts in the maples near,
In the hot noontide, for the music dear
Of my roof-tree birds—but God is good,
And where he is, no solitude.

" Our silent Ernest I sought to teach,
When two years old, the birds' glad speech,
The quail, the wren, the cat-bird's screech ;
He looked where I pointed and shook his head,
He did not hear the words I said.

" Mary, the next, no soulful sound
E'er heard or uttered ; the mole in the ground
Is not more still and fancy-bound
Than she, poor child !—only our Jane
Can hear my words and answer again.

" Jane is married and lives below :
Ernest, the father, under the snow
Was buried ten strong winters ago ;
But life since then has not stood still ;
I journey on through good and ill.

" Change is the winged child of God ;
Lay off, if need, each cherished good,
And thus renew the noble blood ;

As nature gently puts away
Her sweetest shows—her Fall—her May.

"But 'tis not always strife or rest,
Not outward worst, or outward best,
Not north, south, east or west,
That wafts its seasons to the soul,
And leads it to the All-Good and Whole.

"Yon singing Pine's majestic crest
Looks now as when I saw it first;
Yet every beam and breath have nursed
Its constant bloom, and to the seer
'Tis other than it was last year."

Filling her apron with her stock
Of herbs, she said, "The mallows and dock
Grow southward; a cleft of the rock
Shelters the blood-root; and fennel sweet
And winter-green you *there* will meet.

"Here's bitter that will give you health;
There's sweet that takes the life by stealth;
And this I call 'old woman's wealth;'
It soothes the nerves and coaxes sleep;"
And she gave me of it to drink and keep.

See there, "God's Smile!" it almost girds
Our mountain's base—and hark, the birds!
How endless then are His wise words!
"Sunbeams and breaths"—to appear again
In noble lives of women and men!

THE SHAH.

NAY, said the Persian, you are wrong ;
We are the centre ; earth stands still,
And the sun and stars revolve at will
    Round and round forever.
The Shah in the midst stands up erect ;
We and the Shah are the Gods' elect,
    All things were made for us.

O regal Persian, had you eyes
On your grand height, for what goes on
Beyond the Shah's dominion,

Well might you open them !
'Tis good to look at you and smile,
Though we plume our wings and say the while,
Look here, what a mistake !

'Tis but the breach of an old command,
To covet for self what's made for all,
The meanest of sins since Adam's fall :—
Let us not laugh at it !
How many stand up and say in effect,
We and the Shah are the Gods' elect,
All things were made for us !

O Sun, that sweetly laughest o'er all,
O winds, that of the open heaven
Sing to us morn and eke at even,
Patience, bear with us long !
We are not base, we are but dull—
Plead on, till human souls are full,
And match your light and song !

REASONABLENESS.

Would but the sun shine,
  Would but the rain cease,
Would but dear Iris come—
  Then would there be peace!

See how the sun shines!
  The rain begins to cease,
Iris herself is here;
  And, prithee, where is peace?

LOUD heart, that sleep'st when the world's awake,
  I pray you sleep now ; go to your rest,
O owl-like and wild, and let me take
The calm and the full delight, that o'er
My quiet room the moonbeams pour,
  Into my arms and unto my breast,
    And ask for nothing more.

All's to gain,
All is to come between us twain!
O never can serve
Fruition and conquered reserve
To feed the soul with a bliss,
So momently waking,
So troubled, but deep as death,
With a surface doubt and an under faith
Over it breaking,—
As this which we feel—as this!

THE CENCI'S DREAM,

(IN THE NIGHT PREVIOUS TO HER EXECUTION.)

COVER me, mother of God, with silence and pity!
Let the noise of the pleaders cease, the jar of their wranglings—
And all the confusion of crowds, the gazing and wonder!
And again, as of old, when the sunshine awoke and laughed through me,
We twain, little brother of mine, little Rocco and I,
Will go each with an arm round the other, out into the fields.

My Rocco, he died, as we know ;—I remember, I shuddered,
And gasped, as if heaven had drawn all its breath in, for horror.
But then he was safe, he and Cristo, no worse could befall them ;
And together they lay, with the twilight upon them, the darkness
Of earth yet unpassed, and white dawnings of peace. But somehow
My Rocco is with me, is here—comes hither to measure
An hour for once by its sunshine.—And, darling, to wander
With thee is so good ! to glide o'er the sunset Campagna,
As if we had wings, and we have,—and gaze in the fire-well
That sucks back the broad day to its heart—and watch in returning

The procreant east, as it slowly heaps up towards the zenith,
Its violet and rose, for a twelve-hour's remembrance and promise
To earth in her darkness !—Such heart-ease I feel, and such gladness !
Thou leadest—I follow—and see, of all fields for reposing,
Thou alightest with me here !—here, where heart's-ease is growing and purpling
The infinite level !—And O, dost thou cover me with it ?
Head, bosom and arms, with the wealth more than regal ?—and leaning
Thy forehead to mine, make better their breath with thine own,
As thou murmurest deeply, "Poor child," O, at that, how mine eyes
Grow dark all at once, with wild tears ! O, what I have suffered,

The angels may know, who can bear it—but never
thou, darling!

"Little sister beloved,—through what paths the Infinite leads us,
That we miss not the beautiful end, which, below our horizon,
Smiles upward to Him, who could guess? his ministers know we,
Nor by presence, nor sign, nor like favor. To one sends he a mother,
With patience and motherly urgings, to mould the young spirit
To faultless proportions, to strength and high-hearted endurance;—
With like end to another, it may be, a father like ours.
Thou hast 'suffered!' O fearful to think, since in hatred, he struck us,
From life and thy side, what tortures and fear may have rent thee!

But round thee at darkest, some pure-eyed intelligence waited,
And anguished to show thee one glimpse of the Highest's arcana.
And if, overwrought and o'ermaddened, thou had'st erred and stumbled,
The Blessed himself would have hastened to lift and forgive thee.
But listen, and know what great joy may be thine in the future!"

O Rocco, thou see'st how my face is all kindled at thine!

"This flower, which thy sweet body crushes, wherewithal too, I mantle
And hide thee from trouble, is only the mortal foreshadow
Of beds of unperishing sweet and contentment, which yonder

In ineffable azure we make thee ;—but in regions of
twilight,
We spread for our father, the rue—great meadows of
rue—
Round and under still, rue—which means sorrow, and
sorrow, and sorrow."

O pity !—some heart's-ease for him, too !

" Nay, listen ! when ages
And ages have told their slow tale in the rock, there
shall haply
Go forth on its timorous venture to heaven, some
breathing,
Sigh of a soul for its lost and never-returning,—
For a love that was trampled, a peace that was mur-
dered, a goodness
Flung back with incredible mockings—and thence-
forth our father,

With gradual change, shall fade from the place of his
anguish ;
Fade thence and grow into light, till the angels who
dwell there,
Distinguish and hasten to meet him. Could'st thou
see, little sister,
How fair he will be in that luminous air—and fatherly
tender ! "

O Christ, may this be !

" If earth nourish one being—an angel
More constant than spring, with its delicate myrtle,
who shall labor
And watch to the end ;—resisting and watching
through darkness,
And wrestling with demons to win him, she shall plant
in his spirit
Some germ of a faith in the ever unchangeable love
And goodness eternal, that, little by little, shall gather,

And grow, and redeem him ;—as, deep in the fire of
even,
Is born the soft ray of the planet, and night through
its silence,
Throbs surely and slow to its fulness of stars. And
thou—
Thou only wilt do this—wilt do it and save him—thou
Angel!"

How I shrieked! how I tore up the stillness! O par-
don, grave judges,
Awful—black-bearded—there waiting to sentence!
but Rocco,
My brother, was here—and whither he went, most
strangely
I saw not. Perhaps he returned into bliss—and it
may be,
He goes to spread meadows of rue—other meadows of
rue—
Rue, under and round, which means sorrow, and sor-
row, and sorrow.

APPLEDORE.

Look northward from this rock and see,
  Half imaged in the dreamy stone,
Two heads—a veiled Eternity,
  A Destiny, stern, cold and lone.

This grimly fronts the aspiring wave,
  And seems to say, Strive as you will.
And lash my brow all idly brave,
  You are a trembling vassal still.

That, with a human softness, nears
  The breathing Sea, and says, O child,
Judge not of life by partial years—
  In me all things are reconciled !

UNDINE.

THERE is a small and daring sprite,
She is three years old to-night,—
Whom I call, La Motte Fouqué,
After your fairy Undine!
Mid her wind-blown tresses, bright
Shifts and plays the captive light,
As the northern morn in fair
Berenice's golden hair;
Clouds, her eyes, which cannot keep
Their sweet lightnings save in sleep;

And about her mobile mouth,
Fresh with north and warm with south,
Importunate for their fees,
Come and go invisible bees.
Would you the magic will resist
Of this elf monopolist?
She is not like Atlas, curled,
Stooping 'neath the gray old world,
But she takes it lithe and bland,
Easily in her small hand.
Spring is hers and summer flowers,
And fair autumn's mellow hours,
And winter, 'mid his hummocks set,
Delights to be her hideous pet.
This is what all people say
Of our charming Undine.

Erewhile I looked upon her face,
And said, It is good, it lights apace;—
Fills with soul as lilies with light;

And, to keep it ever in sight,
Wrote in my heart upon that day
The story of sweet Undine ;
Who roamed at will the idle air,
Empty, alas ! of thought and care,
Till love came, with the old surprise
Of a soul for the elfin eyes.

Better than praise thy tale doth move,
Poet, that singest so well of love !
Thanks, for all that on the earth
Seek the sign of the second birth !
Accept the gratitude I pay,
Thinking of this our Undine.
What Love creates, Love best can teach ;
And as we would that she should reach
Upward, from fruitful hour to hour,
To purity, and sight, and power,
So we would lead her heart to know
The love of all things, high and low ;

The skies, with sun and moon impearled,
And underneath, the common world ;
And make ourselves, aught else before,
Lovely, that she may love us more.

HALF AWAKE.

Ah, working-day life,
Pain, struggle and strife—
Ado and undoing,
Action and rueing ,
Much undertaking,
Yet ne'er a thing making ;
Purposing featly
To break as completely !
What do I live for ?
What do I grieve for ?

Millions like me have lived,
Millions like me have grieved ;
Of each be it said
That earth was his bed,
And there he lay dreaming :
For a day, however it seemed,
He dreamed ;—for a night, he dreamed that he dreamed.

THE WAY APPOINTED.

EASILY moved, easily swayed
    Hither and thither,
As easily hoping
    And dismayed.

Up in the clouds—over the hill,
    Higher and higher,
Down, down in the meadow,
    And lower still.

Shadows over me, far, afar—
Moving and moving—
Dropping my eyelids,
There too they are.

The sun, a golden key I win,
Turning and turning,
Opes the sweet heavens
And lets me in.

Lovers, 'tis true, lovers a score ;
Sighing and sighing ;
One, right one, were better,
Yet, fate, send me more.

Friends leave me, how, I cannot tell ;
Yearning and yearning,
Others rise after,
Loved as well.

In blasted hopes new ones thrive ;
    Joying and grieving,
Ephemerals wholly
    Help me to live.

Mother, she planned—Father with strife
    Planted and watered—
For what, are you asking ?
    To fit me to life.

World, said I, your tasks I do not refuse ;
    Take me and try me ;
Turn me and mould me,
    And put me to use.

Millers the water, sailors the wind ;
    Headfull and heartfull—
You will not ? dull world, you,—
    Then go—never mind.

Vainly I veil—your eyes shoot between ;
    Fairly and frankly,
I am a maiden
    Turned of eighteen.

KRISTEL'S SOLILOQUY.

My log house stands by the river :—
Not higher than the topmost swell
At the vernal flood :—but I have an attic,
And over it stately poplars shiver,
And lend me twenty arms ecstatic
To lift me over the surge. And well,
When the roaring freshet threatens, I know,
And, taking my meat and honey, go
Into the leafy nook above ;
Whence I watch the river, raving
Up from its yellow depths, and the broad

Lagunas, islanding many a grove ;
And if the waters me defraud
Of homestead and home, and turn my cabin
Into a raft,—I do not murmur
More than a thrush, whose nest in summer,
A twisted branch of ash displaces ;
For are there not a million places,
And leaves in the wood for the minstrel free,
And a million logs as well for me ?

Such is my manhood's outer shell.
Over many a flowery swell
I follow the trail to hunter dear.
The plain's long-bearded nobles rear
Their ponderous fronts, and snuff with doubt
The air my rifle scatters about.
Whether at midnight or at noon,
At the hour beloved of the rising moon,
When the deer come forth from their shady lair,
I watch by the licks, or in the dark

Recesses of the wilding park.
From wood and field, and flood and air,
Treasures of beauty and of use
My lowliness do not refuse.
The summer robe of the bison falls
In shady softness down my walls ;
The stag's coat hides mine earthen floor ;
His antlers, branched like a sapling oak,
Are cornices for window and door.
And plumes that tropic winds have strook,
In tapestry of varied thought,
By hands of forest maidens wrought,
Come to my cabin, without strife
To live again in a human life.

And yet I wage no needless war ;—
No wanton hand strikes down the wing,
Or stays upon the bended plain
The bison's stately journeying.
No form of lowliest grace I mar ;

Nor in the forest's wide domain,
Nor in my garden's round, I cull
Aught good, or sweet, or beautiful,
But all the more to dedicate
To service pure its gentle state.

True, in a corner of my hut
Is a little shrine, whereon I put
Fresh-blooming children of the wood—
Forget-me-not and the solitude-
Shunning linnæa. Unto the same,
I consecrate the winged flame
Of columbine, and that which stole
The innermost secret of the sky,
The water-lily's vestal soul,
With the sweetness in the clover hived
So deep. This is in memory
Of one, whose love my love outlived.
And so, to steep
In memory all that I should keep,

The queen magnolia there I set,
And circle it with low mignonette.
For I think ofttimes, altho' her sphere,
Radiant and high, I come not near,
Nor ever can again—that still
If I surround her thought with love,
And evermore a patient will
To watch, to strive, to wait and prove
The peace heaven offers, to the end,—
Out of my pain and silent strife,
Some fragrance God will take, and blend
An unknown sweetness with her life.

The prairie sways, and the river rolls,
And the sun and the moon—and nothing is lost
In all the skies' unmeasured coast,
Nothing too in the kingdom of souls.
Bròad stream, that yieldest silently
Such largess to the noonday sky,
Hear how the brooding cushat mourns

Her love. We will not mourn or weep,
Or lock ourselves in wintry sleep ;
But bide in peace heaven's large returns.
All that he has and is, who gives,
With whom no earth-born wish survives
To hoard his little grief or bliss,
God his great debtor surely is,
And pays infinity. Who meet
The coming fate half-way, and fling
Their blessed treasures at her feet,
Shall feel, through all her clamoring,
Her hard eye quail ; she knows 'twere vain
To empty what God brims again.

TWENTY-SECOND OF FEBRUARY.

In bygone days when we were weak,
  Some strong men by us stood,
Like primary rocks to front the storm
  And buttress the infant wood.
Then we had Adams, and Otis, and Lee,
  Then we had Franklin and Jay,
Then we had Washington, kingman of all;
  Great names—great men were they.

There were baby truths in those old days,
  And there was full-grown wrong;
They smote the last with iron blows,
  And helped the babes along.

Chivalrous times and men were they—
  Hearts of the grand old breed,
Gaston de Foix, and the Knight *sans peur*,
  And Roderick the Cid!

What did they know of party bribes?
  When did they kneel to pelf?
And when were country, and man, and God
  Less in their deeds than self?
Were the mountains taller in those days?
  The streams more swift and strong,
That they caught the trick of a nobler grace
  And of a manlier tongue?

Northern aurora, speed your light
  Into our skies' cold gray,
Appeal to the glad to-morrow
  From recreant to-day!
O shame this backward-looking glance,
  O shame this paltry fear,

And men of might, be men of faith,
  Far-eyed, deep-eyed and clear!

Valor is valor over the world.
  Ah! do not think to gain
The hero's glory and meed of praise,
  Without his wound and pain.
'Mid well-won palms, earth's sovereigns sit
  On high in joyful calm,
But a bleeding heart is in each one's hand—
  A heart for every palm.

Past days,—past men—but present still!
  Men who could meet the hour;
And so bore fruit for every age
  And amaranthine flower;
Who proved that noble deeds are faith,
  And living words are deeds;
And left us dreams beyond their dreams—
  And higher hopes and needs.

Not often great in name or place,—
  Great but to think and dare,
Some steadfast eyes yet look to truth,
  Some steadfast hearts watch there.
And when they speak or when they sing,
  Strange music seems to rise,
But the angels know 'tis the burthen old
  Returning to the skies.

CAMILLE.

I BORE my mystic chalice unto earth,
  With vintage which no lips of hers might name :
Only in token of its alien birth,
  Love crowned it with his soft, immortal flame ;
      And 'mid the world's wide sound,
  Sacred reserves and silences breathed round
  A spell, to keep it pure from low acclaim.

With joy that dulled me to the touch of scorn,
  I served : not knowing that of all life's deeds,
Service was first—nor that high powers are born

In humble uses ;—fragrance-folding seeds
Must so through flowers expand,
Then die :—God witness that I blest the Hand
Which laid upon my heart such golden needs!

And yet I felt through all the blind, sweet ways
Of life, for some clear shape its dreams to blend ;
Some thread of holy art to knit the days
Each unto each, and all to some fair end,
Which through unmarked removes,
Should draw me upward, even as it behooves
One whose deep spring-tides from His heart descend.

To swell some vast refrain beyond the sun,
The very weed breathed music from its sod :
And Night and Day in ceaseless antiphon,
Rolled off through windless arches in the broad
Abyss.—Thou saw'st I too
Would in my place have blent accord as true,
And justified this great enshrining, God !

Dreams!—Stain it on the bending amethyst,
 That one who came with visions of the Prime
For guide, somehow her radiant pathway missed,
 And wandered in the darkest gulf of Time!
  No deed divine, thenceforth,
 Stood royal in its far-related worth—
 No God, in truth, might heal the wounded chime.

O how? I darkly ask.—And if I dare
 Take up a thought from this tumultuous street
To the forgotten Silence, soaring there
 Above the hiving roofs, its calm depths meet
  My glance with no reply.
 Might I go back and spell this mystery
 In that new stillness at my mother's feet!

I would recall with importunings long
 Her so sad soul, once pierced as with a knife;
And cry, Forgive! O think, youth's tide was strong,
 And the full torrent, shut from brain and life,

Plunged through the heart, until
It rocked to madness, and the o'erstrained will
Grew wild, then weak, in the despairing strife.

And ever I think, What warning voice should call,
Or show me bane from food, with tedious art,
When love, the perfect instinct, flower of all
Divinest potencies of choice, whose part
Was set 'mid stars and flame,
To keep the inner place of God, became
A blind and ravening fever of the heart!

I laugh with scorn that men should think them praised
In women's love;—chance-flung in weary hours,
By sickly fire to bloated worship raised!
O dream long-lost, so sweet of vernal flowers!—
Wherein I stood, it seemed,
And gave a gift of queenly mark;—I *dreamed*
Of passion's joy aglow in rounded powers.

I dreamed ! The roar, the tramp, the burthened air
  Pour round their sharp and subtle mockery.
Here go the eager-footed men—and there
  The costly beggars of the world float by,
    Lilies that toil nor spin—
  How should they know so well the weft of sin,
  And hide me from them with such sudden eye ?

But all the roaring crowd begins to make
  A whirl of humming shade :—for since the day
Is done, and there's no lower step to take,
  Life drops me here. Some rough, kind hand I pray,
    Thrust the sad wreck aside,
  And shut the door on it ! a little pride,
  That I may not offend who pass this way !

And this is all ! O, thou wilt yet give heed !
  No soul but trusts some late, redeeming care—
But walks the narrow plank with bitter speed,
  And, straining through the sweeping mist of air,

In the great tempest-call,
And greater silence deep'ning through it all,
Refuses still, refuses to despair.

Some further end—whence thou refitt'st with aim
Bewildered souls perhaps—? Some breath in me,
By thee, the purest, found devoid of blame,
Fit for large teaching—? Look, I cannot see,
I can but feel !—Far off,
Life seethes and frets, and from its shame and scoff,
I take my broken crystal up to Thee.

ARIADNE.

SHAME on these tears! disown them, lofty heart!
On this bald peak where now I stand alone,
Like some poor weed, sea-driven and flung apart,
Bear witness all ye Gods, that I disown
Their traitorous record!—Yet nay, let them run
Into the deep-mouthed wave—and take along
Memories I want no more;—soft, rustling throng
Of old, untold delights, pass, every one!
With empty arms outstretched, I cry, O sea,
That took so much, take these!—see there! I fling
The clinging warmth of that first kiss to thee,
The pulses' lingering lightnings, that they bring

Unto this bitter, burning soul no more
The wild renewal of that past delight,
When love sprang sudden to its perfect height,
Unfolded sweet, yet fearful, like a flower
'Neath the mute throbbings of the conscious night!

Pass, pass, as ravings of a drunken soul!
Yet, Gods, who rule this empty, awful world,
Who mete to highest and meanest things their dole,
Ye know no sight more fearful than one hurled
From some great joy into a doom of pain
O'er-deep for fathoming—no sight save this,
Of a proud heart that flings away all bliss
Of hope or memory; nor asks again
The friendly shadow of some little grief,
Or some sharp pang, its numbness to o'erbear,
But lightning-proof and desolate, a leaf
Left living and alone in wintry air,
Meets feelingless and dumb the evil wind,
Nor cares what woes are laboring up behind.

Still, still a sickening sense creeps o'er me. Still,
O Tethys, whose mad daughters, every one,
Clap their white hands above the waters dun,
My heart is like thy waves, that proudly fill
And roar, yet bound and break when all is done.
Speed, bitter droppings, to the bitter sea !
All worthiness is gone, all memory
Of truth, and nobleness, and charity !
And I, alone, and pressed by this great void,
Bend shameless to the earth with unalloyed
And boundless wretchedness. I am no more
Than a dull snail left houseless on the shore.
Hide me, O pitying Gods ! Ay, let me find
Some wind-wrung peak or cataract-gated cave,
Whose thunderous roof through the dread years shall bind
These throbs to silence !—This, O fearful Powers,
That send the black, inexplicable hours,
This, or the dear and all-forgetting grave !

SIESTA.

THE old apple tree,
Noblest on the hill—
Takes me in its arms ;
There I lie a-dreaming,
Dreaming at my will.

Birds and birdlings chirping,
Think not I am there—
While they trill wild notes,
Think not of my dreaming
In the scented air.

(Pray you do not mark !
I pray you shut the doors
On your fine brains—be sure
'Tis only foolish dreaming,
Unfit for wits like yours.)

Leaves glance light above—
Boughs beneath me yield,
Moving like long waves,
Or golden rye a-dreaming
On a July field.

My eyelids softly closing,
Rarer sights I see ;
While all the outer music,
All the gay leaves' dreaming
Seem to follow me.

Feeling, scarcely thought,
Old sweet grief and mirth,

Like gold fruit are hanging,
'Mid green boughs of my dreaming,
Far above the earth.

Hope and bird-eyed fancy
Midway chirp and sing;
A rainbowed mist of music—
A hum of cherubs' dreaming—
The sound of blossoming.

Peace, a deeper peace—
Joy, a fuller tide,
Like swans on glassy waves
Come gliding down my dreaming,
Gently side by side.

Say you, little wren,
That our life of mirth
Distances a king's,
As the sky in azure dreaming
Distances the earth?

Well said !—Noisy world,
Custom's weedy throng,
Here I give the go-by—
For they match not in my dreaming
With your wing and song.

Hearken, little bird !
When God, round your heart
Laid those mottled wings,
He gave you heavenly dreaming
For your life-long part.

I, my wild translator
Of that upper bliss,
On my doubtful pinions,
Fanned through some strange dreaming,
Ere a dream like this.

THE CRICKET TO OCTOBER.

THE long, pure light, that brings
To earth her perfect crown of bliss,
Wanes slow—the thoughtful drooping of the grain,
And the faint breath of the earth-loving things
Say this.

Oft when the dews at night
Clasp the cool shadows, all in vain,
I look along the meadows level dark
To see the fire-fly lift her tender light
Again.

From the thick-woven shade,
Where, on the red-cupped moss to-day,
A crimson ray alit, the blue-bird sends
One melancholy note up the brown glade
This way.

Last night, I saw an eft
Crawl to the worm's forsaken bier,
To die there, as I think :—beetle nor bee,
Nor the ephemera's ethereal weft
Sport here.

Yet great has been life's zest.
Almost how the grass grows, I know,—
And the ant sleeps ; the busy summer long,
I have kept the secret of the ground-bird's nest
Below.

But sweeter my employ
In some still hours. I seem to live

Too near the beating of earth's mighty heart,
Not to have learned in part how she can joy
And grieve!

'Twas on a night last June,
Into the clear, bold sky,
The little stars stole each with separate thrill,
And the mossed fir-top woke its mystic rune
Close by.

Upon yon westering slope,
Two glorious human shapes there stood,
Rosy with twilight, listening to my song:
I knew I sang to them of love and hope,
Life's good.

The little stars' soft rays
Again thrill through their realm of peace;
One shadow haunts the slope,—a song I sing
To match the broken music of her days—
Then cease.

Dim Eden of delight,
In whom my heart springs upward like a palm;
Loving your morning strength, your evening calm,
Your star-inspired Night—
A sweeter breath blows upward from the sea,
Like a fresh hope from God's eternity;—
Latest and best, are you then coming?

Nay—shadow is not here;
Save of the rocks upon the gleaming sands,
And that which moves beside me with clasped hands,

A suffering shadow, drear
With watching, it would seem, the endless swell,
Great, white-faced waves, sent ceaselessly to quell
The stern and silent shore with thunder.

TEMUR.

When Temur, chief of Omars, died,
God's angels bore his soul away
Unto full-flowered Paradise :—
There, as the Persian prophets say,
No flower shall feel decay—
Perpetual are the splendid skies.

But Temur was a tyrant fell :
And Seyd, whose fair first-born had known
The terrors of the Despot's sway,
Murmured, as on his eyelids shone
Rays from the burning throne,
Whitherward oped the angel's way.

But God, the just, who now and then
Speaks in the soul's emphatic dream,
Took Seyd the murmurer, that night,
And led him to Kur's wakeful stream,
Which lay in the moon's beam,
Blooming with lilies of her light.

There curved the mountain line away ;
And there, the murmuring lapse of blue
Let in between green silences,
To ripple the level smoothness through ;—
And 'mid soft light and dew,
Temur's hushed palace rose into the skies.

What life in every peaceful thing !
What trance of living, joyful might !
The heavens may breathe it unto men,
And bulbuls by the charmed light
Sing it to sacred night,
But who may utter it again ?

Seyd saw the open, blooming heaven ;
And the rich well-springs of the air
Fresh'ning the overburthened world ;
And o'er dark brows of guilt and care,
The intermitted peace—God's fair,
Soft-visioned Night of night unfurled.

" All Beauty is of God the good ;
Yon scarf of stars his angels wove,
And earth is sweet of Paradise ; "
He mused ;—" O wretch, that would'st remove
Aught from his saving love,
Or stint his patient ministries ! "

THE WILD PLUM TREE.

You should have seen it, sire ; a vicious thing,
   Knotting defiance in its crabbed twigs,
   And arguing with full fifty bitter leagues
Of sea-winds maddening on a rocky shore.

No wonder ! well, half-doubting I uptore
   And bore it inland—doubting, set it here,
   Where it might feel the garden's warmth and cheer,
And only heaven's forbearing winds might come.

Only its attic vigor to maintain,
  I fed it each quick-blooded spring
  With salt to thirsting, and it grew, my king,
Straightened, and bloomed, as never plum before.

Here is the fruit. So please you, taste and see
  How nature straight replies to such a call;—
  And yonder has my plum, beneath the wall,
The warm earth colonized with fruitful trees.

RAPHAEL MENGS AND HIS "HOLY FAMILY."

So reverently he treads
This home where heaven is,
That you the steps might hear
Of the very angels near,
Almost as soon as his.

Pure breathing of a soul
Whose depths we only guess,
Since unto it was given
To know so much of heaven,
So much he could *express!*

Gazing, the old ideal,
Paler, more rapt and still,
With sadly wondering eyes,
Just dips from her far skies,
And shames my laggard will.

Humility and love,
Perfume of lowliest sod—
I yet can think that they
Winged our close world one day,
And went untouched to God.

SEASIDE.

Go wear your tortured smile ; speak and say nought ;
   Be laughed at by your diamonds—I prefer
My light, loose garb—freedom of face and thought,
   And this uncompromising thunderer.

What do I where you mince and compliment,
   And meet to hide the better, and deny
The deeper life within you ?—I was sent
   To live at least in simple verity.

For your poor, famished lives of ostentation,
  What victims bleed of which you never recked !
The yearning heart of love—the aspiration
  Which makes us royal, the sweet self-respect.

But ah ! I know the lonely hour will find you
  Sincere once more ; to-night doth sadness wait
To fold you in her purple, and remind you
  Of your dead strength, your regal, lost estate.

THE GRAVE-DIGGER.

As pleasant a man as you would see,
  Native or foreign, to vouch I dare ;
His laugh was hoarse but full of glee,
  Indifferent when or where.

But most in graves the old man kept
  His singular jubilee ;
He roared at what most others wept ;
  His life was a funeral glee.

He had no rival in his trade :
  He knew, one after another,
All the village would need his axe and spade,
  And troubled himself no further.

His love and duty were never at strife—
  His charity looked to all ;
He seemed to think his lease on life
  Long as death held carnival.

He reasoned, " Well, 'tis nature's creed
  And man's chief want—is burial."
The friend of the world in its sorest need,
  Could the world then spare him well ?

EPITAPH

INSCRIBED TO RICHARD, WHO LOVES NOT THE SUBJECT.

HERE lies,
(Speak softly,) one who dropped away
As a ripe berry from the spray;
She ended nine lives in a day.

Just at the sunset, as a spark
Winked by the firelight, did her bark
Put forth into the unknown dark.

She had no kin to stay her breath ;
As lonely traveller hasteneth,
She swam for life the moat of death.

All musings of the fireside born,
All love, all fear of hate and scorn,
The rose of life and its sharp thorn,

These have exhaled ; in dumbest show
'Twas willed the curious life should blow,
And, having blossomed, should pass so.

Ah, not unkindly does the grave
Shut out earth's sunlight, if it have
The power to ripen and to save.

But you, O cat of many years,
When the inevitable shears
Cut off your thread of hopes and fears,

Tell us, what hope could love supply ?
What page of drear philosophy
Would say thou didst not vainly die ?

"As the beast dieth," holy writ
Remorselessly hath worded it,
And so constrains our feeble wit.

Poor beasts ! in mild Chaldaic lore,
When shepherds watched on starlit moor,
Your destiny was not so poor.

Great Nature to her open feast
Gave welcome wide, the highest guest
Had common birthright with the least.

To live to die ! it could not be ;
Birthright was immortality :
Yea, what was born could never die.

Alas, what better faith have we ?
What light of heaven shines tenderly
On this dark web of mystery ?

What shall we say of what was here ?
A thing that held its life as dear
As one of us, in hope and fear.

Dumbly it asked for human care ;
A little love, that it might bear
The ills and pains it could not share ;

Some patience for misdoings small ;
For dulness, ignorance, and all
That made it a dependent thrall

On human kind. Perhaps not dumb,
(Nay, Richard !) in new guise shall come
Into the spirit's older home,

This poor dependent of our hearth,
Linked with old scenes of peace and mirth,
Or cruelty, and pain, and the bleak earth.

MEMORY.

A THING that glideth about
When the stars are in and the sun is out ;
Escaping and cheating the eye
That seeketh it out most anxiously ;
Yet when the night-shades fall,
And the work of the day is done,
Ever it trippeth home
By the light of the evening sun.

DOMINIQUE.

A SWEET hope fluttering at my heart
  Seems oftener like despair,
A treasure, never yet confessed,
  Turns fair to foul, and foul to fair.

Because I may not hope this hope,
  This feeling may not feel,
Its joy has boundless aim and scope,
  Its fiery pain no touch can heal.

Gather me roses with the thorn,
  And berries with the bane ;
Blend into one the night and morn,
  Blend summer's sun with wintry rain ;

Yet these are never like the woe,
  The treasure I conceal ;
All bleak, all dark, all bane, all thorn ;
  My fiery ill is all my weal.

SONNETS.

NIGHT.

I.

O calmly, lovingly, Night, vast and deep,
Bend round the breathing world ! Thou cool-browed
wife
Of fiery Day—he, stirrer of old strife,
Thou, soother, mother, in whose heart we keep
A hiding-place to dream, to hope, to weep !
Who still exhalest in the purple sky,
The old star-bloom of immortality,
Wreathing our momentariness and sleep
With dignity so sweet and sovereign !
Happy the earth to kiss thy broidered hem !
Her weak and flagging aspirations take
New pinions in thy shadows ; thou dost make
Love deeper bliss, and even care and pain
Are great and worthy, since thou touchest them.

II.

THOU seem'st to solve the eternal unity
That holds us all. How far, and dim, and deep,
Bathed in the separate sanctity of sleep—
Lost in thy wide forgetting do we lie!
O, lest that dim abyss, where Memory
Beats her disabled wing, and hope is not,
Point to yet wilder deeps, unearth our thought
In thy far glances! Through the serene sky,
When Day from the impurpled hills furls up,
And heaven's white limits fail, the Infinite,
Long crushed within, breathes forth its mystic pain
From vast of height, and depth, and silence, stoop,
And lift with mystic faith its brow again,—
Call unto peace the eternal child, dear Night!

III.

DARKNESS surrounds me with its phantom hosts,
Till silence is enchanted speech. I feel
Those half-spent airs that through the laurel reel,
And Night's loud heart-beats in the tropic coasts,—
And, soaring amid everlasting frosts,
To super-sensual rest, as it might outweigh
A whole world's strife, o'er me gaunt Himaleh
Droops his broad wing of calm.—Those peaks, ghosts
Outstaring Time, through darkness glimmering!
No rush of pinion there, nor bubbling low—
But death, and silence past imagining;—
Only, day in and out, with endless swing,
Their aged shadows move, and picture slow
One on another's unrelenting snow.

IV.

O HIGH-BORN souls, such as God sends to mould
His ages in—and you too, who have known
The pang of strife, and are at last at one
With nature so,—yea, all who have made bold
Our timid dreams, and proffered to the hold
A certain joy—come mingle in life's cope
Star-fields of verity and stable hope,
With these swift meteors and illusions old!
I sent this summons through the deeps of june,
When life surged up so warm and affluent,
It wrapt the very whiteness of the moon;—
No wonder many came—they came and went—
And thou, who sleep'st half sad and wak'st with pain,
Thou camest too and dost alone remain.

V.

So reed-like fragile, in the world's whirl nought,
Beggared in earthly hope, alone and bare,—
Heart pierced, wings clipped, feet bound, but grandly
 there,
Ay and with odds 'gainst Fate, thou standest, fraught
With courage to know all !—Thus is thy lot
Worlds deep beneath thee.—Lovest thou that keen
 air ?
Thou ask'st not hope, nor may the falsely fair
Approach thy clear integrity of thought.
Such power, what shall we call it ? For this time,
Not love, nor yet faith ; but Eternity
Dilating the mean Day,—the spirit, free
And self-reliant, from its purer clime
O'erruling earth, by spirit-law sublime—
God cleaving *for* thee the remorseless sea.

VI.

Of better fortune coming, then, talk not,
Thou teachest, and think not :—nay, rather dare
The utmost of the world's ill strength, despair.
Take up with courage the unlovely lot,
And it shall grow in thy familiar thought
To beauty.—Dumb sorrows that the life-strings wear,
And stings—the points of broken trust, and care,
And those hot, random arrows, whose keen shot
Must find thine or another heart, shall all
Be rounded in the sweet and ample sky
Of the enfranchised soul. Eternity
Shall come home to the hour.—Thou didst not call
Light, light—heaven, heaven—till now, when not a thrall,
But king thou art—yea, free, forever free.

VII.

In the still hours, a stiller strength was born
Deep in my heart.—It was no selfish dream,
Nor even hope, with far and tender beam,
To make me for the moment less forlorn:
Nor was it child of will, before the morn
To dream itself away. With life dismayed,
God help me, O God help me!—so I prayed;—
A simple prayer, but winning swift return;
A hand, that raised all gently from the dust,
And led me childlike on, beyond the strife
Of vulgar aims, past anguish and distrust,
And the pale warders of our daily life,
To where God binds above our harvest sun,
All fragmentary being in his one.

VIII.

Stoop low, dear Night, a little star-breeze wakes
The solemn pines.—Child-love doth come and pass,
And when 'tis gone, how beautiful it was
We know. "Thou art like this dear Night, that shakes
Her long hair down, and sits star-throned in lakes
And loving seas," he said—forgive the boy!
"And you are gold-tressed Day, the sun-flower's joy,
Each each pursues—but neither overtakes."
"O dull astronomer, do not these two
Mingle at dawn and even with lovely grace,
Till one for joy dies in the long embrace?"
Experimental science is sole true;
And like those twilights 'mid the arctic snows,
The dusk and fair blent sweet on cheeks and brows.

IX.

O NIGHT, a terrible dismay still lurks
In thy close caves. Is there another grief
Than mine upon my soul, or spectral leaf
In the great record of the years, where works,
Not dreams, find place—a task declined
Which the wise heavens appointed for my own
Nay, or a haunting memory to strike down
The future's open hand ;—then, down the wind
With sadly human eyes, but fanged like wolves,
The pale Erinnyes sweep. O happy, then,
If I with night-long prayer may win again
Lost faith—faith in Eternity that solves
Time's stoniest spectres—faith in the broad
Serenity of things—yes, faith in the good God !

X.

When my friend went, half-stunned, I thought,
Great God, what then has fallen from me? Power
to feel
The sun, after the three days' storm—to kneel
Before the sacred presence in the wood,
Or by the throbbing sea—to shun the brood
Of slave-besetting ills? But more, more went.
I did not know, the fearful bow once bent,
What arrows it could send:—still, all is good;
What am I, God, to say, spare this and this?
The rain-drop moulds a world. Turning, I knew
Thy pulse in one still, patient love, that drew
Me sweetly upward ever, like a kiss;
Like him, who, sinking in his lonely hour,
Found heaven within the desert's single flower.

XI.

WITHIN my life another life runs deep,
To which, at blessed seasons, open wide
Silent, mysterious portals. There reside
These shapes, that cautiously about me creep,
This iron mask of birth, and death, and sleep,
Familiar as the day and open-eyed ;
And there, broods endless calm. And though it glide
Ofttimes beyond my sight, and though I keep
Its voice no more, I know the current flows
Pulsing to far-off harmonies, and light
With most unearthly heavens. The world but throws
A passing spell thereon—as winter, bright,
Pale feudatory of the arctic Night,
Swathes with white silence all these murmurous boughs.

XII.

YET are there sunbeams, though the kingly sun
Reveal not his full eye ; yet flowers, to bear
Mute witness of the Heart that keeps the year,
Through all its wintry chill ; and I have won,
Where was no face nor voice, a glance, a tone,
A spirit, call it, that all shapes doth wear,
And brings me knowledge which I scarcely dare
Call mine. Now, out of grief it sings ; anon,
It calls me in another's deed or word.
Capricious is the sprite, and now will herd
With common things, now wing me wind-warm cheer
From far-off times and climates happier,
And when from distant fields I call the bird,
A quiet chirp proclaims it nested here.

XIII.

I KNOW this spirit bridges unknown space
And half-forgotten centuries, that I
May know I am of royal family,
And live to my high birth. The marble face
Of Destiny grows fluent, as I trace
These arteries of broad being. I can wait
More years than earth allots me, for my state
Is not of time : nor binds me any place,
Since on and on the mazy current tends,
That takes my little thread, a breath might sever,
To mingle it with universal ends ;—
And tho' I fail and fall, yet am I still
Most strong ; since every high, tho' balked endeavor,
God intertwines with his eternal will.

XIV.

Alas! and yesternight I woke in terror,
Crying, Great God, what awful shadows press
Around us from this dreary nothingness
Of death, and life's old, caverned glooms of error!
Are we immortal, Father, are we dearer
To thee than common dust? "Thou art but one
Of this dense throng, through time still hast'ning on;
Thy blood with theirs is warm," my good Familiar
Said softly unto me,—"how canst thou slake
Thy thirst when their lips parch, or rightly see
With twilight misting round thee? Dearest, wake!
Thy brethren are not saved except in thee;
Nor thou, save in their health, their joy, their sight,
Hast any lasting peace, or heavenly light."

XV.

O MANKIND'S God ! most silent and most lowly
Is wisdom's entrance to our hearts ; with less
Of conscious power, than self-forgetfulness
And an enduring patience ! Though most slowly,
Thou winn'st us by such lovely paths to know thee,
And the immortal life that from thee flows.
But if thy mild lure fail, come untold woes,
Doubt, pain, and learning's poor, convicted folly,
To make self bitter, and compel us forth.
We *live* not in a part ; our prophecies
Are infant wailings—wailing of the earth !
Only the ocean matches the great skies—
Only the infinite of love and ruth
Receives the living infinite of truth.

THE FUGITIVE-SLAVE-BILL.

DEAR God, who art so very calm—
All-seeing and so patient still,
Fill me with calm before thee ; root
From out my heart, the germ and shoot
Of narrow sight and selfish will.

And though my heart impatient beat,
And bitter tears I stem within,
May I recall that life to-day
Of pitying Christ, which seemed to say,
The saddest of all griefs is sin.

O patient souls, that sadly toil
Where bleeding feet before have trod,
The oppressor and the oppressed are here ;
I know you choose the weight, the fear,
The stripes above the awful rod !

We talk of sorrow—talk of death,
Old signs for old things all unmoved.
Who bears about this deadly grief,
An inward bane, with no relief—
He only grief and death has proved.

What wonder, if men sometimes doubt
If God be in his heavens or no ?
The lightnings open them, but still
And fine, the motions of his will
That keep true balance flit in veins below.

No little thing that seems to live
Its poor, mean life, a creeping clod,

But has a hope for its brief hours,
A joy perhaps more fine than ours—
A something it may keep from God.

In silent ways, He evens all.
All silently, the mean he brings
Up to his own transcendent height:
All silently with inward blight,
He shrinks oppression's evil springs.

But go not thou, with truth like this,
To the poor thralls of grief and fear,
Till thou hast labored well and long,
To heal their wounds, to right their wrong,
And won the noble right to cheer.

And who may close his eyes and hands?
You, if the air's free motions breed
No joy in you, if you may vaunt
To live without a hope, nor want
Man's comfort in your bitter need.

Our rivers, from their mountain springs,
Deepen and broaden to the sea ;
And ever as they stream along,
Warble their noble mountain song
To meadow lily and tulip tree.

Forget your native hymn alas !
And be to earth's warm breast as dead—
Or breathe one breath of Freedom's morn,
One blast upon her mountain horn,
And let men know where you were born and bred !

No narrow policy—O no—
East, west, north, south alone to suit !
No chartered wrong—no "fixed fact" lie—
No mean to-day's expediency—
Seed of to-morrow's bitter fruit !

O not beneath God's light, forego
Your birthright in our dear-bought land !

Your freeman's reverence for the free,
Your freeman's faith in liberty—
Your freeman's unslaved soul and hand!

And if man bid you darken life,
Quench hope and seize what God's love gave,
Leave the poor serpent to his hiss,
Do aught, be aught, but be not this—
Far rather be a *southern* slave!

FACTS IN VERSE.

Bring here thy loom ; and lay the warp
All through of gold : with silken thread,
In violet, yellow, black and red,
As another, tones upon a harp,
Thou improvisest lovely shapes,
And reëmbodiest the dead.

My words I know no grace can vaunt :
 But thou, within thy magic loom,
 Wilt give them meaning, strength and bloom,
And the tale I tell shall have no want,
 Pictured in fadeless sun and gloom.

A speck here, journeying to the west,
One sees a mount with beetling top,
The very plunge of the wave, when drop
The flashing curls from its sharp, white crest.

Soon you come to the mountain land ;
Where peak beyond peak in their cloud abodes,
Like Titans at rest and at peace with the Gods,
The ancient, beautiful brethren stand.

So calm and sane are they, we know
When there, no more of the babble and strife,
The passion or emptiness of life,
We are up with them, and the world, below ;

Above the belts where summer clings ;
Where silence ever wakes and broods
Around their wild and vapory hoods,
Low rustling its enchanted wings.

We listen through their clinging mist,
  For hymns in far-off childhood heard ;
  Old hymns of faith, from those that guard
The snow and the sacred amethyst.

Thou dost not feel their music cease,
  When at thy feet, some little bloom
  Smiles suddenly from covert gloom,
And minds thee of a lowlier peace.

Those threaded sunbeams of the wood,
  The wildering rivulets, merrily
  Kiss thine intruding feet and flee,
As careless of thy higher mood.

Gold green the blessed valleys lie ;
  By giant shadows now embraced,
  And now with sunbeams interlaced,
And panting 'neath the happy sky.

If here and there the smoke upcurls,
  It witnesses of some warm hearth,
  Where nestle human loves and mirth,
Gray eld and sunny boys and girls.

Among those regions fair and dread,
  A fallen trunk's majestic beam
  Bridges a granite-walled stream,
An hundred feet above its bed.

So brief the space from ledge to ledge,
  Only the mid-day sun can send
  An arrow that its depth may rend—
And three steps on the sturdy bridge
  Will span it clear, from end to end.

A maiden, on a summer even,
  Stood there above the torrent's flow,
  And looked into the depth below,
And up the hollow sphere of heaven,
  As if to measure some great wo.

Her birth-place, circled with soft air,
  Lay many a league away :—her kin,
  Her mother of a darker skin,
Who called, in pride of her fair hair,
  The pretty maiden, Lilian.

None knew her history—nor he
  Who loved her, guessed what phantom dread
  Mocked at her heart's young feast, and said,
Mid fragrant woodpaths, up the free,
  Bold hills, " Be evermore afraid."

Forgive her that she did not clear
  Her soul of the great weight it bore ;
  And for its silence ached the more ;—
The heart made weak with earthly fear,
  Love cannot teach it all its lore.

At length the ill foreshadowed came ;
  And hope called home its latest beam.

She caught one day the evil gleam
Of keen and cruel eyes—the same
That turned to nightmare childhood's dream.

Was it strange that thoughts of death should then
Fill all her soul ?—but with calm pace
She turned her from the trysting-place
That night ; (what wonder, yet again,
Is death the darkest thing to face ?)

And wending homeward thro' the even,
She stopped above the torrent's flow,
And looked into the dark below,
And up the empty, silent heaven ;
And could not measure her great wo.

The waters kept a merry din ;
From peopled wastes and wilds untrod,
And brightly over love's abode,
The perfect day shut softly in,
The wondrous Passion-flower of God !

She said, I thought this world so wide!
With room for every hope inwrought
Here with the life,—Love, Freedom, aught
To lesser creatures not denied;—
Simply, I knew not what I thought!

When the owl leaves his hollow tree,
He ofttimes captures on the wing,
Some poor, belated, panting thing,
A little thrush, perhaps, that free
Fares homeward 'mid June's blossoming.

I envy, God, that little thrush!
He is not hated of his kind;
I envy him his free-born mind,
And last, his home foregone—the hush
Of absence that he leaves behind.

When with my love, I sought the Fall
But now, and over wave and bird

His low, assuring speech I heard—
I thought that I would tell him all—
For love is better than its word.

But no, God, no ; for as I live,
'Twere death and worse, to watch alone
The gradual change come dark'ning down ;
How tell him that I sought to give
To him, what never was my own ?

But now if from his path, at length,
I glide like last night's pleasant dream,
Which could not wait the morning's beam,
Though memory has its bitter strength,
The sweet too stays to comfort him.

God pardon me my selfish heart !
But is it not best then to be
A clear strain broke—a memory
Of good alloyed not, as thou art,
Bird, to home watchers in the tree ?

'Twere good then, when to morrow's sun
  Comes with its slow inspiring on,
  To be one sacred ray withdrawn—
A sweet want in the heart of one—
  A silence through the waking dawn.

Yonder, great heaven, men wait to bind
  These limbs with chains ! the night-birds roam
  To seize the loiterer wending home !
'Tis well, they are not of my kind,
  For I am human, let them come.

* * * * * *

The jubilant waters far below,
  Went harping over twig and stone,
  And roots with black moss overgrown ;
One scarce had noticed in their flow
  A slightly changed and muffled tone.

One only, who forbidden still
 To follow her, said in heart-play,
 I will haste round the longer way,
And while obedient, have my will,
 And see her once again to-day.

He waited long beside her door,—
 Then said, Her foot is swift and light;
 An hour ago, if I read right,
She passed this happy threshold o'er—
 He stooped and kissed it 'neath the night.

And laughing at his vigil vain,
 And thinking, when the sun's gold edge
 Should ripple over the eastern ridge
Of clouds, they two would meet again,
 He loitered homeward by the bridge.

There listening, Is it mists of night,
 That break thy murmur to my ear,

Or pausest thou, shuddering with some fear,
Or burthened with a new delight,
Dear stream, thy voice is not so clear?

Perhaps through wood and rocky reach,
A spirit of the wave, thy bride,
Runs softly wimpling to thy side,
And thou, confused in thy speech,
For painful joy dost talk so wide.

When love with love makes God's clear day,
A light for every coming year,
Each thing to hope and fancy dear,
Comes double laden, or, best say,
Is half a joy and half a fear.

So feeble are we! and the fair,
Sweet Presence that within us sings,
The hour, that like concentred springs,
Comes freighted with its heavenly air,
Cannot forego its heavenly wings.

He, musing as his pathway led,
  Met comrades from the field's late task :
  A happy lover what can mask ?
Not night or silence : greetings said,
  Your Lilian, she is well? they ask.

The calm, far starlight healing fell
  On scarred trunk and broken ridge,
  And seemed to give an answering pledge,
As he replied, My love is well,
  We parted yonder at the bridge.

Nor was he mindful of love's cheats,
  Till they had passed, when, smiling gay,
  He thought, In sooth, I did not say
Amiss ;—love still is near—and meets
  And parts, a thousand times a day.

So passed he homewards, weaving dear,
  Soft dreams and hopes in garlands slight ;—

What thrilling touches of strange light,
What breaths from some far atmosphere,
World, in thy grand, old pause of Night!

Spirits that watch, do you not pray
In the still hours, Light come no more,
Shine not upon life's blasted flower—
Let only us see it, who may
See God and earth, the self-same hour!

Doubt, terror, the long agony
Of dread suspense, sore ill to brook!—
Until on many a fearful nook,
The sun sends in his searching eye,
And looks there till he makes men look!

Believe that there are times so rife
With vital blood, as many say,
That moments ere they pass turn gray,
And fruitage on the vine of life
Ripens and drops in one brief day.

God keeps us :—that is something good,
  Whichever way the current run !
  When Fate its sorry worst has done,
He leads you to life's marble mood,
  Where, torpid, you await the sun.

But if, as may be, God unlock
  Despair with lightning, you shall turn
  In vain some kindly rest to earn :
The soft, south wind your pangs will mock—
  The very stars will sting and burn.

Bethink thee, if thy soul's true mate
  Should sudden from thy side be caught,
  With last eve's kisses newly fraught,
And darkness overhang his fate,
  A mystery that deadened thought ;

And doubts, that first had plied their wings
  In covert of the twilight gray,

Should wing at last the open day,
And doubts should grow to whisperings
That you had reft that life away ;—

"O God !" you say, "they left him so—
Widowed of all men's love, to grieve
And die"—? Nay, worse than that—believe
Time's shuttles fly ; we scarcely know
The awful pictures he may weav

They crippled first his manly strength
With prison air and prison gloom ;
And ere mid-winter's frosty bloom,
From chains and judgment-bar, at length
They gave him to the felon's doom.

What said he—what he thought—God knows !
A fear, a frightful doubt, ere long
A dread belief of some deep wrong
Done, in the minds of men arose,
And waxed from day to day more strong.

And then there came from the south land,
  Sealed, as men say, with dying breath,
  Confession as from hell beneath,
That two, who waited near at hand,
  Had seen the wretched maiden's death.

"Gone's gone, lost, lost"! Say you, I mar
  With sadness life's most heavenly things?
  'Tis but the air that sweeps the strings;
You cannot probe the earth-mould far,
  Ere you shall reach her tearful springs.

Dear, skilful lady, in whose loom,
  The breath of natural joy and pain
  Is woven, as nerves are in the brain,
A crimson gush wraps all our room,
  The close of Day's triumphant strain!

Is it the coming night-breath, wreathed
  With phantom dews, that all those wan

Acacia flowerets seems to fan,
Or the living joy through nature breathed
By the infinite hope of man ?

SONNETS.

CONTINENCE.

I PLEDGE you in a cup not overbrimming.
Though heirs to all, God knows our weak hearts best,
And tempts us gently from our downy nest,
To the wide air. Yon fresh horizon, dimming,
And tempering to our thought, the abysses gleaming
Beyond ; eternity's severe, pure light
Soft prismed by time ; and love, the infinite,
Through human founts intelligibly streaming,
Teach us that heaven withholdeth but to fill :
Grasping thou would'st lose all. Wait then and see,
In the old press of duty steadfast still,
How comes the unexpected god to thee ;
How the wild Future, that now mocks thy clasp,
Lies trembling in the Present's nervous grasp.

TO THE SPIRIT.

BY A PRODIGAL'S FAVORITE.

Thou teachest better things unto my heart,
Than with my mouth I sing. I would fain be
The Memnon of the sunrise that I see :
I would the uprising flame would dart
Forth from my lips in living melody.
Or might I mock that inward hymn—! In vain ;
Like the poor bird that seeks so passionately
To breathe its rival's more melodious strain,
I beat my wings for nought. And yet, O soul,
Life, love and nature, better thus to live
With you in close embrace, as whole in whole,
Than to give happily with less to give ;
I drink continually the nectar up,
Yet never see the bottom of the cup.

TO THE SAME.

BY A MISER'S PENSIONER.

ONCE, spirit, as a little child, I went
Unto the burning mount, where thou didst stoop
To pluck me from low cares and sorrows up,
My inspiration, my abandonment.
Thou camest, because the messengers I sent
Were love and noble longings. I was given
To that self-losing which restores us heaven.
But now my sacrificial robe is rent,
And turns to ashes in the poisonous breath
Of this low life—and fast contract mine eyes
To meet the glare of colored vanities.—
In passionless self-possession croucheth death ;
Better than this were agony and strife—
Wake me to life, if need be, bleeding life !

C. L'E.

I DWELT content with God and loving all,
In those first years; but ere long, something strove
Within—and, Fame, I thought, is larger love;
And love of fame, in every noble soul,
Is love of love;—and, though I missed the goal,
I could but see how, quite beyond our wills,
Some pure and deep Intelligence fulfils
Our longings in its own deep way.—My shoal
God centred in a starred, unfathomed well;
The world might roar at will; 'twas charity
Merely to let it go; around me fell
Surpassing sun and air; and for earth's free,
Broad paths were slight, restraining arms so pale,
And endless kisses by the yearning sea.

THE SAME.

'TWAS then we said, thrice happy in our earth,
That when ripe summer in the cornfield stirred,
And brought its mother instinct to the bird,
Silent within the boughs,—there should go forth
An unsuspected power of good, to girth
The world with more enduring beauty, since
Two lives should then grow one, for furtherance
Before all things, of ends of godlike worth.
Now . . I know not. . . God's way is scarcely clear;
Perhaps earth could not clasp so great a good,
And heaven takes up the trust . . still, work is here,
And something dearer in the springing sod
Than was of old, when all was very dear—
And so once more, but more alone with God.

From all these mounds, though day blows fresh and warm,
The wasting snow of this snow-haunted spring
Marks out her nameless hillock ; lingering
As loth to rifle of its virgin charm,
That spot of all. No sudden-winged alarm
The little blue-bird takes, that looks abroad
From yon top twig, with prophecy o'erflowed
Beyond all dread or heeding ;—hark ! so calm
Rills forth his vocal sunshine on the air !
A frail hepatica has here forerun
The bounty of the season.—Ah, forbear !
Take no life here : the aspiring dust has won
To other bloom and sweetness—let us share
With God's mute confidant this vernal sun.

THE SAME.

MIGHT we make quest, through this soft circling sky,
In whose wide breath that little breath was lost,
Which sweetened all our air, for the dear ghost,
It were in vain, we know :—but happily
When the poor frame dissolves, the spirit high
Makes it her messenger to the elements,
Which tell us by unnumbered fair events,
What the heart yearns to know : aye, to the sigh
Of ever-questioning love, even heaven unbars
Joyful, its azure-gated mystery,
And says, Who wings a thought, poor though it be,
From his meek distance upward to my stars,
Is linked to God in whose great thought they are,
And his imperishable life must share.

THE PASSION FLOWER.

THE cross, the thorns, the cruel nails again!
Thus opens God's diviner flower of Day
To thee, Flower-giver: was no better way
Found out, whereby thou early should'st obtain,
What others seek through life-long years in vain,
Peace and a large, sweet charity, than this
Which that stern angel points thee to, whose kiss
Of consecration on thy brow is PAIN.
I weep consenting—knowing well that so
God tempers to a more than mortal fineness
O Friend, so high in sorrow—be not mindless
I keep for thee a heart-warm rest below;
With hopes and human yearnings, wilt thou know?
It shall not mar thy strength or thy divineness.

www.ingramcontent.com/pod-product-compliance
Lightning Source LLC
LaVergne TN
LVHW011223110826
845150LV00006B/1518

9781425515812